Introductior

The signs welcoming visitors to S
entering a 'Saxon hilltop town'. Su
hints at the depth and breadth of history that is about to unfold before
them – more than 1,100 years of continuous and at times eventful
history. At 705 feet above sea level, Shaftesbury is also the highest town
in Dorset by some margin, with spectacular views across most of the
county and parts of the adjoining counties of Somerset and Wiltshire.

Shaftesbury was effectively founded by King Alfred the Great, who
built a Benedictine nunnery here in the 880s and installed his young
daughter Æthelgifu (or Ethelgiva) as the first abbess. His twofold
purpose was to provide a fortified refuge for people in the event
of more Viking raids like those that had punctuated much of the
ninth century, and to revive the monastic ideal that had been all but
extinguished during that same period. Shaftesbury Abbey went on to
become one of the biggest and wealthiest nunneries in the country,
controlling vast estates across much of Dorset and Wiltshire. It was
also the last to go in 1539 when another English king, Henry VIII,
ended six and a half centuries of monastic domination through the
Dissolution of the Monasteries.

With the abbey church and nunnery buildings reduced to building
stone for later generations of Shastonians, a new phase began for the
Saxon hilltop town – a phase that still has almost 200 years to run if
it is to match the nunnery's 650-year lifespan. While the nunnery's
destruction was the greatest and most dramatic event in Shaftesbury's
long history, change did not stop in 1539. Like every other town,
Shaftesbury continued to evolve and still does.

In *Shaftesbury Through Time* we attempt to reflect the changes
of the last two centuries through 'then and now' pictures and
informative captions. Compiling such a book is a fascinating task
but it also presents many challenges. Streets that once provided a
safe playground for children, an easy thoroughfare for horses and
wagons and a picturesque backdrop for late Victorian and Edwardian
photographers are now coated in tarmac, littered with street signs and
in many cases lined by descendants of the motorcar that was in its
infancy when those photographers were at work. In some parts too,
trees and shrubs now obscure buildings and views that were more
readily visible in the past.

Despite these challenges, writing this book and taking the 'now'
photographs has been an enjoyable task and something of a voyage of
discovery. Although I have known Shaftesbury all my life, and have

a genuine fondness for it, I have had to educate myself in the finer points of its history and geography. I could not have done this without the resources of the Gold Hill Museum and its army of volunteers, especially Ray Simpson and Claire Ryley. Ray and Claire have devoted many hours to the search for appropriate pictures and information about them. I am also indebted to the authors of other books on Shaftesbury, whose knowledge and insights have proved invaluable, in particular Brenda Innes (*Shaftesbury: An Illustrated History*), John Chandler (*A Higher Reality: The History of Shaftesbury's Royal Nunnery*), Eric Olsen (*Images of England: Shaftesbury*), F. C. Long (*Tales of Old Shaftesbury*) and Laura Sydenham (*Shaftesbury and Its Abbey*).

Ray, Claire and I are also grateful to the many others who have contributed in various ways, particularly my friend Barry Cuff for the loan of twenty Shaftesbury postcards from his Dorset collection; Phil Yeomans and the Bournemouth News and Picture Service (BNPS. co.uk) for the 2013 Hovis re-enactment; Peter White for information about Shaftesbury Workhouse and the gasworks; Kathleen Heasman and Jane Stacey for information on the St James's Street fire; paramedic Steve White for information about the former gasworks site; and the many people who have given information about their properties or simply agreed to stand in a certain location to help me recreate a photograph.

Roger Guttridge

SHAFTESBURY
THROUGH TIME
Roger Guttridge

AMBERLEY

About the Author

Roger Guttridge was brought up in Sturminster Newton just 8 miles from Shaftesbury, where his father Tom worked as a telephone engineer from 1951 to 1974. He has been a journalist in Dorset for forty-eight years, writing for most of the county's newspapers and magazines. He is well known for his features and columns on Dorset history and is the author or co-author of twenty books, including *Dorset Smugglers, Dorset Murders, Ten Dorset Mysteries, Blackmore Vale Camera, The Landscapes of Dorset, the Villages of Dorset, Paranormal Dorset, Sturminster Newton Through Time* and *Dorset: Curious and Surprising.*

First published 2018

Amberley Publishing
The Hill, Stroud, Gloucestershire, GL5 4EP
www.amberley-books.com

Copyright © Roger Guttridge, 2018

The right of Roger Guttridge to be identified as the Author of this work has been asserted in accordance with the Copyrights, Designs and Patents Act 1988.

ISBN 978 1 4456 6449 1 (print)
ISBN 978 1 4456 6450 7 (ebook)

British Library Cataloguing in Publication Data.
A catalogue record for this book is available from the British Library.

Origination by Amberley Publishing.
Printed in Great Britain.

Shaftesbury from Melbury Hill

The highest town in Dorset is famous for its views and here are two from the outside looking in – both taken from Melbury Hill more than a century apart. The 1785 drawing (above) is by Samuel Oram Marsh, an attorney as well as an artist and poet, and was published by High Street printer Thomas Adams. The church towers of Holy Trinity (left) and St Peter's are the dominant features on the skyline but the cottages of Gold Hill and St James's Street can be clearly seen along with the heavily developed area around the High Street and The Commons. Cows, horses and a handful of people occupy the fields in the foreground. Below, a similar view in the early twentieth century shows additional development here and there, most notably the Town Hall to the left of St Peter's Church. Grazing cows dominate the foreground and behind them to the left is what appears to be a large tent.

Abbey Ruins

But for a strategic decision made by King Alfred the Great, Shaftesbury might even today be just another of the many green hills that define much of Dorset's landscape. After repelling Viking invaders in 878, the Saxon monarch launched a programme to create a series of fortified 'safe places' across Wessex, where his subjects could take refuge and defend themselves in the event of further attacks. At Shaftesbury he combined this with another aim, to revive religious values, by establishing a Benedictine nunnery at the heart of the fortified town and installing his young daughter Aethelgifu (or Ethelgiva) as the first abbess. This was in the 880s and for most of the next 650 years Shaftesbury Abbey flourished as one of the biggest and wealthiest nunneries in the country. Above: an aerial shot of the abbey ruins looking towards the town centre *c.* 1960. Below: looking south across the abbey ruins, Park Walk and the Blackmore Vale from the tower of Holy Trinity Church on Gold Hill Fair day 2017.

Abbey Ruins

At the height of its influence, Shaftesbury Abbey had more than 100 nuns. By the time Henry VIII dissolved the nation's monastic institutions, that number had halved, although it was still the biggest and richest of England's 137 nunneries and the last to be closed – on 23 March 1539. The last nuns included Dorothy Clausey, the illegitimate daughter of the late Cardinal Wolsey, Henry's former chief adviser, who was persuaded to keep her parentage under wraps. By 1548, according to contemporary surveys, most of the abbey church had already been demolished while by 1574 the associated convent buildings had also been 'laid low to the ground'. The stone from the Norman rebuild around 1100 provided a handy source of material for Shaftesbury builders. Only fragments of the once grand abbey church survive today, uncovered in various excavations since 1816. In 1931 the abbey made international headlines after the discovery of a casket containing the skull and half the skeleton of a young man, presumed to be those of the teenaged King Edward the Martyr, whose remains were brought to Shaftesbury after his murder at Corfe (now Corfe Castle) in 978 by his stepmother. Edward's shrine became a magnet to pilgrims for centuries but the bones left Shaftesbury after the site changed hands in 1951 and, despite legal attempts to have them returned, the bones were eventually rehomed at a Russian Orthodox shrine in Surrey. Above: the ruins looking east in the 1930s with St Peter's Church in the background. Below: looking south-east today. Inset: A 1548 sketch of the ruined abbey church with the former Holy Trinity in the background.

7

Park Walk

The abbey complex covered a much larger area than we can see today: a schedule dated 1565, less than thirty years after the Dissolution of the Monasteries, listed forty chambers and a similar number of ancillary buildings. The nuns themselves lived and worked in the area we now know as Park Walk. A recent geophysical survey revealed the outlines of other buildings under the tarmac. Park Walk itself has changed little in 120 years but the view of Holy Trinity tower and the Westminster Memorial Hospital are now largely obscured by trees and extensions that are best described as architecturally challenged.

Pine Walk

From the old picture, it's easy to see how Pine Walk – the footpath that connects Park Walk with Love Lane and St John's Hill – acquired its name, but you'd be hard-pressed to find even a single pine tree today. The Walk is a convert to the deciduous and should perhaps be renamed Beech Walk – although walkers seem to be almost as scarce as pines. The line of Park Walk is today believed to follow the line of King Alfred's earthen defences on the south side of the Saxon town.

Laundry Lane and Stoney Path

The above view of St James's from Park Walk includes a fine display of laundry, appropriately hung out to dry in Laundry Lane, which connects to Stoney Path and Tanyard Lane. This may be a coincidence, although this part of Shaftesbury has an age-old tradition in laundering. In his eighteenth century *History of Dorset*, Revd John Hutchins noted that Laundry or 'Lander' Lane ran from Park Walk down to St James's parish, and that in a garden at the bottom was a well called Laundry Well. Here the linen from the convent was probably washed, he reports, adding that 'the Laundry House is pulled down but the well is still in use'. Below: Most of the old Lander Lane is now known as Stoney Path but its route has not changed since nuns trod it daily 1,300 years ago.

Laundry Lane and Stonehaven

The 1930s woodcut by Shaftesbury's High House Press shows the L-shaped thatched cottages that formerly stood at the end of Laundry Lane, probably on the site of the original Laundry House that Hutchins refers to. The building was destroyed by fire during the Second World War. The story goes that a woman jumped from an upstairs window and was caught in a blanket by people from a nearby pub. Stonehaven (below) was built on the site in 1953 using stone from the fire-ravaged building, plywood bomb cases to line the roof and tiles 'robbed' from Tyneham, the abandoned Dorset village that was famously requisitioned by the government during the Second World War and never given back. Recent owners believe the site of the old Nuns' or Laundry Well is in the corner of the garden.

St James's from Park Walk

Park Walk was laid out as a fashionable promenade in the 1760s and given to the town in 1815 by John Dyneley after the death of his landowner brother Robert, who intended to extend the walk to Castle Hill but died before he could complete his plans. Many of Park Walk's original sycamore trees were felled in the 1950s after storm damage. From its south side, Park Walk offers fine views of St James's, the Blackmore Vale and some of Dorset's chalk hills, although as in many locations the lower parish is today partially obscured by trees and bushes.

Hospital and War Memorial, Park Walk

The Russian cannon that stood at the junction of Abbey Walk and Park Walk more than 100 years ago was captured during the siege of Sevastopol in 1855 during the Crimean War. It remained a popular attraction among children, passers-by and photographers until melted down for armaments during the Second World War. The war memorial now stands where the Victorian lamp standard was. Many centuries earlier, the abbey's pigeon house stood close to this spot. The oldest part of the Westminster Memorial Hospital (built in 1871) is today largely obscured by trees.

Gold Hill, Early 1900s

Following the destruction of the abbey in 1539, the hub of Shaftesbury life moved a few yards eastwards to the area where Gold Hill meets the High Street and The Commons. Picturesque Gold Hill's steeply sloping cobbles, imposing abbey wall, curving terrace of ancient cottages and view of the vale and hills beyond have combined to make it one of the most famous and photographed streets in not only Dorset but the whole country.

Gold Hill, Early 1900s and c. 1995
References to Gold Hill or 'Goldhulle' occur as far back as 1350. In ancient times sheep and pigs were penned on the hill on market days. The house (top left) stands on the site of the former Lamb Inn and a forerunner of the workhouse until it was rebuilt around 1900. The picture below features former Shaftesbury town crier Stanley Mansbridge (right) and a colleague from Wimborne on a Gold Hill Fair day in the 1990s.

15

Gold Hill: the Hovis Years

In 1973 a TV commercial for Hovis bread thrust Gold Hill into the national consciousness. To a soundtrack of Dvorak's 'New World' symphony and an old chap reminiscing in a northern accent, a flat-capped bread delivery boy is seen pushing his bike to 'Old Ma Peggotty's' at the top of Gold Hill, then freewheeling down with legs akimbo. The forty-five-second commercial (left), directed by a young Ridley Scott, won several awards and more than thirty years later was voted Britain's favourite TV advertisement of all time. In 2013, Carl Barlow, who was a thirteen-year-old stage school student when he played the Hovis boy forty years earlier, returned to Shaftesbury to switch on the Christmas lights, and was again photographed on Gold Hill with his bike (below). The retired fireman returned again in 2017 to film a video promoting cycling – this time with an electric bike. Tourists continue to recreate the scene today.

Gold Hill and Town Hall

Six years before Hovis came to town, Gold Hill featured in several scenes in *Far From the Madding Crowd*, the 1967 film based on Thomas Hardy's novel of that title. Gabriel Oak, played by Alan Bates, is seen walking up the hill while Sergeant Troy (Terence Stamp) precariously leads his red-coated cavalrymen down the cobbles. In the film's most moving scene, the rag-clad Fanny Robin arrives, weak and exhausted, at the workhouse door, where a few hours later she dies during childbirth along with her baby, fathered by Troy. At the top of the hill once stood the ancient Gold Hill Cross – probably a preaching cross and one of at least six crosses that once existed around the town – with stocks alongside. The cross was removed in 1826 to make way for the present Town Hall.

Old Market Hall, *c.* 1790, and Town Hall, 1840

Most of the 'old' pictures in this book are photographs but on these two pages artists of yesteryear offer their impressions of the High Street. Above is a drawing by 'Buckler' showing the Old Market Hall that stood alongside St Peter's Church from 1550 until 1820, when it was demolished for road widening. The open-arched ground floor area provided shelter for market stallholders while the Town Council met in the room above. The present Town Hall was built in 1826 and its entrance porch and railings can be seen (far right) in the picture below, drawn in 1840 by Clarence Rutter. The traffic includes two stagecoaches and a water cart (far right) but it's quiet enough for the locals to have a gossip mid-street. In the foreground four birds peck away watched by a four-legged mammal. They look more like hens and a lamb but are presumably pigeons and a dog. Drawing animals was not Clarence's strong point.

High Street, *c*. 1850, and a 1909 Cartoon

The *c*. 1850 picture above again shows the new Town Hall next to St Peter's. The oblong platform next to the carts in the foreground is something of a mystery. Enlarged, it looks like a stone platform with a row of large pots and a kettle. It could have been a collection point for water brought up from Enmore Green or perhaps a Victorian sales point for food and drink. The unusual postcard below, by H. E. L. Brickell, was drawn in 1909, when the first flying machines were starting to appear, and anticipates how things might be five years hence. 'What is coming to Shaftesbury AD 1914,' reads the main caption. The location is the High Street outside St Peter's Church. Across the skyline is an assortment of aerial craft including a passenger plane above a 'landing stage'. Posters advertise flights to Blandford, Sherborne, Yeovil, Twyford, Marnhull, Duncliffe, the Stours, Gillingham, Motcombe and Fontmell. 'Aeroplanes for Stour etc leave from Castle Hill,' says one poster. 'Aeroplanes for Melbury etc. leave from The Park,' says another. Long-haul travel was well beyond Mr Brickell's imagination.

High Street, and Market Hall Arch, Bell Street

The main photos above and below show the High Street from The Commons in the early 1900s. Above, a trail of horse dung reminds us of the main mode of transport 120 years ago. The archway a few doors along on the left was the entrance to the Market Hall, which ran through to Bell Street, where a second arch (inset) is now the main entrance to the Arts Centre. Auctioneer John Jeffery had an office in the Market Hall, which was also used for drama productions and film shows, among other activities. Below, several large barrels can be seen outside the Town Hall. Could these contain water brought up from Enmore Green or beer for a Gold Hill or High Street pub? The original wooden clock tower was built in 1879.

High Street, Early 1900s

Above, a large crowd has gathered to watch Shaftesbury's Edwardian photographer Albert Tyler at work as a couple of lads with ladder and chair make themselves at home against the lamp standard, which has appeared since the mid-nineteenth century sketches on the preceding pages. The shop on the far left corner was Strange & Sons' boot and shoe shop. Below, St Peter's Church and the Town Hall dominate the street scene in an unusual colour postcard from the era before the motorcar. St Peter's is one of only four survivors of the twelve churches that existed in Shaftesbury around 1300, the only one that was not rebuilt by the Victorians and one of only two still used for worship. It was extended in the sixteenth century.

High Street, c. 1914 and Today

The uniformed troops lined up in the High Street are described on the postcard above as 'Kitchener's Army', indicating that they were volunteers who had responded to Herbert Kitchener's famous plea for recruits in the First World War. The card is postmarked 1916 but the picture may have been taken as early as 1914. You can't help but wonder how many of these recruits did not live to see their home town again. The white building towards the far right was the draper and outfitter Robert Gutsell's shop. When poor Mr Gutsell arrived in Shaftesbury at the beginning of the First World War, he had to place newspaper advertisements to counter suspicions that he was German – he was not. He also made a significant contribution to the war effort and his own son, Leslie, was killed in 1916. Below is a similar view from the Town Hall balcony on a sunny Gold Hill Fair day in July 2017.

High Street, *c.* 1930 and *c.* 1950

As we move through the twentieth century, the horse-drawn traffic has given way to the internal combustion engine while the many shops continue to change hands from time to time. But the Victorian or Edwardian lamp standard and its 'Keep left' sign survive in the two pictures on this page, which date from around 1930 (above) and around 1950 (below). Adjoining St Peter's is the Mitre Inn, a historic pub that was rebuilt in the twentieth century. The two single-storey structures outside the Town Hall were public toilets.

High Street towards The Commons

The High Street looking towards the restaurant known as King Alfred's Kitchen in the 1950s with the Mitre Inn and St Peter's Church on the left. The bus on the left is bound for Gillingham and is advertising Cerebos Salt while the double-decker on the right is the No. 24 for Bournemouth. Also on the right are Lloyds Bank and Frisby's Shoes, both of which could be found in most high streets then. In the modern picture, sunlight illuminates King Alfred's Kitchen and adjoining Nature's Treasures as dark clouds approach from the west.

The Commons from Town Hall, *c.* 1960 and 2017

King Alfred's Kitchen and The Commons from the Town Hall balcony in around 1960 and on Gold Hill Fair day in 2017. With their Tudor beams, bay window, broken roofline and other 'olde worlde' features, the restaurant and neighbouring shop present one of Shaftesbury's most prominent and historic buildings, and they stand at a location that is even more historic. In the days of the abbey, this was the site of the Broad Hall, which fronted on to the medieval marketplace and dispensed food and drink to the poor.

Grosvenor Arms, 1840, and Semley Hollow, *c.* 1900

Clarence Rutter's sketch (above) of The Commons in 1840 was drawn just fourteen years after the Grosvenor Arms (right) changed its name from the Red Lion following a rebuild and Earl Grosvenor's acquisition of much property in the town. The Rutters were and still are a well-known Quaker family in Shaftesbury. The corner shop on the left is marked 'Rutter, bookseller and chemist', with Rutter's Printing Office above. John Rutter, the first of the family to settle in Shaftesbury, also ran a public reading room and subscription library and later trained as a lawyer. To the left is the shop of Watts, importer of wines and spirits. In the background is the then new Town Hall with its railings and distinctive arches. After the opening of the Salisbury to Exeter railway line in 1860, the Grosvenor started a coach service to and from Semley station. Below, the horse-drawn Grosvenor coach makes its way up Semley Hollow in the early 1900s. The road is now part of the A350.

The Commons, *c.* 1920 and Today

It's now around 1920 (above) and the Grosvenor Arms has traded its horse-drawn coach for a motorbus, while Rutter's across the road has become the post office. In the foreground there is obviously some work going on around the lamp standard, and the adjacent pump and wet road suggest it may have something to do with water. Since 1840, the smaller building to the right of the Town Hall has been replaced by Hill & Boll's Motor Works and Garage (later Pike's). More rebuilding has gone on since then and the present structure houses several businesses, including Blackfoot's gift shop. The Grosvenor Arms will soon enter its third century under this name while the former Rutter's shop, and post office is now Sloanes Bespoke Hair with the HSBC bank next door.

High Street, Early 1900s and Today

The middle section of the High Street looking towards King Alfred's Kitchen in the early 1900s and today. Almost every business has changed hands, an exception being Lloyds Bank (the tallest building in the middle distance on the right), although even this was the Wilts and Dorset Bank until Lloyds took them over in 1914. The building with the attic windows (near right) is now the Edinburgh Woollen Mill, but the Georgian three-storey building between it and Lloyds Bank has been replaced by the entrance to Swans Yard and a rather less aesthetic post-war structure that is home to Superdrug, solicitors Blanchards Bailey and estate agents Connells. The sign on the left is advertising 'hats and caps', perhaps part of John W. Bragg's clothing business advertised on the next sign along.

High Street and High House

The lower High Street from the junction with Mustons Lane around 1900 and today. The buildings and rooflines have changed little in 100 years but every business has changed hands, in most cases more than once. The shop far right in the old picture was Mr Baker's china and fancy goods store (with a selection of brooms outside) while second on the left was Gatehouse, saddler and harness maker. The aptly named High House on the right formerly housed the High House Press, founded by James Masters in 1924 and famous for its high-quality hand-set printing and book production. It also printed this (inset) and other fine woodcuts of Shaftesbury. High House Press products continue to be sought after by collectors. The shop on the corner of Mustons Lane is now Chaffers, estate agents.

High Street from Angel Square

Looking up the curving lower High Street from Angel Square, the pair of cottages next to Shooters Lane (far left) were demolished many decades ago and replaced by what is now Cranbornes gift and fashion accessories shop. Most of the other buildings on both sides have changed only superficially in 100 years or so. Like most shops, the Cranbornes site has had many trading incarnations including a fruit shop, fish and chip shop, music shop and electrical store. A few doors up on the right we can just make out the low white frontage of the Picture Palace.

High Street Picture Palace

The classically fronted Picture Palace, pictured (above) in around 1920, opened in 1914 and was Shaftesbury's first cinema. During its construction a skeleton was found on the site. It was medieval and associated with nearby St Martin's Church, which has since been demolished. The Picture Palace closed in 1925, when the Market Hall further up the High Street was converted to a cinema and called the Palace. The old Picture Palace site is now occupied by the British Heart Foundation charity shop. The shop next door, which was Reg Humphries's cycle and motorcycle shop in the 1920s photograph, is now Bargains.

Angel Lane

The surviving thatched cottages opposite the present-day police station make Angel Lane eminently recognisable despite the passing of time. The nearest cottage has lost its thatched roof, probably in a fire many decades ago. It was originally two terraced cottages and is now a hairdressing salon called Makuti – which means 'thatch' in Swahili! The Cedars Nursing Home opposite was formerly Cedar House, home of builder O. Cutler.

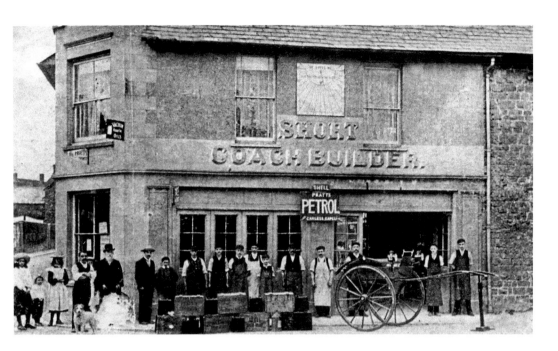

Angel Square

The post office at the corner of Angel Lane and Coppice Street was once the site of the Angel Inn before becoming Philip Short's coachworks (above). Smiths, body-makers, wheel-makers, painters and others worked in various workshops, showrooms and stables. A house also stood on the site. A sundial high on the post office wall is the only visible survivor of the previous complex. It was originally erected in memory of Dr Evans, who was fatally injured here in 1897 aged thirty-six. The GP was driving his carriage with his seven-year-old son alongside when his horse bolted, overturning the four wheeler and throwing him against a wall. He had a fractured skull and broken thigh and died twelve hours later. His son landed on him and escaped with bruising.

Coppice Street Looking East

The view looking up Coppice Street from Angel Square presents a very different picture today than it did more than a century ago. The terrace of thatched cottages (near left) have gone, replaced by the telephone box and the edge of the post office yard. The children in the background are standing near the turning into present-day Charles Garrett Close and the entrance to Tesco.

Coppice Street Looking West

Looking along Coppice Street towards the town centre, the stone wall on the left has survived but much else has changed. Even those thatched cottages that survived have mostly traded their reed roofs for tiles. The site of the pretty cottage near right was a building site when the modern picture was taken.

Salisbury Street and Angel Square

The above view of Angel Square from Salisbury Street is one of the earliest available, probably dating from the 1890s. The pavement on the right is still cobbled while the dresses of the ladies on the left are late Victorian. In the background, Short's coachworks can also be seen to the right of Angel Lane. The shop near right was Burden's Corn Factors and is now Parfitt's shoe shop. Below, workmen prepare to lift a steel drainage pipe into the trench with part of Angel Square again in the background.

Salisbury Street

Angel Square from Salisbury Street today. The entrance to Angel Lane is a good deal wider than it was in the days of Short's coachworks. The view below looks along Salisbury Street from Angel Square in the early 1900s. The shops on the left now include a solicitors, a shoe repair shop and the butchers Prime Cuts.

Knowles Arms, Salisbury Street

The pub on the right of the old picture was the Knowles Arms, which owed its name to a bitter election dispute in 1830. After Earl Grosvenor's nominees defeated Reformers candidate Francis Charles Knowles, and celebrated with extravagant feasting and drinking at the Grosvenor Arms, Knowles opened his own pub and carriers business and called it, with unsubtle irony, the Knowles Arms. The pub and the adjoining Spiller's Almshouses were demolished in the 1970s and their sites redeveloped. The houses opposite have changed very little in 100 years. The railings between them mark the entrance to the former Ebenezer Hall, a Nonconformist church building nicknamed the Tin Tabernacle. Just out of shot (left) is St Edward's Roman Catholic Church (inset), opened in 1910.

Old Cann Rectory

A stone's throw from the former St Rumbold's Church, formerly the parish church of Cann, are the Old Cann Rectory and Rectory Gardens, now private residences. For thirty years of the twentieth century, this was the home of the Revd N. S. Lawrie, described by F. C. Long in his book *Tales of Old Shaftesbury*, published in 1979, as a 'jolly parson and very much esteemed'.

Shaftesbury School

The oldest of Shaftesbury School's buildings in Salisbury Road dates from 1878. In the above picture, taken around 1910, when it was Shaftesbury Grammar School, boys can be seen doing military drill, which was then a standard part of the curriculum. The school traces its origins to 1718 and has accepted boarders since 1898. It is now one of only thirty-eight state boarding schools in England. It converted to academy status in 2014 and now educates 1,300 boys and girls. The picture below dates from c. 1900. Inset: A close-up of Shaftesbury Grammar School c. 1915.

Shaftesbury School and Old Cann Church

Standing almost in the shadow of Shaftesbury School's Victorian building in Salisbury Road is the former Cann parish church, otherwise known as Shaston St Rumbold's. It was built in 1840 on the site of the previous church, renovated in 1910, and now houses the offices of the Southern Academy Trust, an amalgamation of several schools that includes Shaftesbury School. Until recently the church served as the school's drama studio.

Butts Knap

The fingerpost sign and lamp standard at Butts Knap have been replaced by the Cann war memorial. The road to the left is Salisbury Road while the right turning is Lower Blandford Road, much realigned at this point following construction of the Royal Chase roundabout. As its name suggests, this was originally the Shaftesbury end of the lower route to Blandford, now part of the A350. The present-day entrance to Shaftesbury School is just out of shot on the right. Behind the wall (far left) is The Mount, home of former GP and Liberal politician Dr Geoffrey Tapper. Many years ago this house had farm buildings and acres of fields stretching up Christy's Lane almost to the top end of Coppice Street.

Old Cann School, Salisbury Road

The Old Cann School, left of the old picture, taken after a snowfall, is just about visible behind the hedge next to the traffic sign in the equivalent view today. The school was built in the 1840s, closed in the 1960s and is now a private residence. The wall opposite was removed as part of the Royal Chase roundabout development and a second access to Lower Blandford Road was created (far right). The building to the right is Butts Mead House, part of the Butts Mead development built in the grounds of Cann House, which was demolished forty or fifty years ago. *Inset*: the opposite views on the same snowy day over 100 years ago and today. The footpath in the foreground was originally part of the Salisbury Road.

43

Old Toll House and Royal Chase roundabout

The Old Toll House or Round House stood at the former junction of the Salisbury Road (left fork) and the Higher Blandford Road (right). The Toll House was demolished half a century ago to make way for the Royal Chase roundabout, which now occupies the site. At the same time this access to the B3081 Higher Blandford Road was closed off and a new junction created a few yards further along the A30. The Tollhouse was once home to the Weldons, a show family who took their hand-powered fairground rides to local fairs along with Mrs Weldon's popular gingerbreads. Just off the roundabout is the historic Half Moon pub (inset), parts of which are hundreds of years old.

Belmont House and Royal Chase Hotel

The Royal Chase Hotel pictured in 1891 when it was a private house, and today. It was built in the early nineteenth century by James Barrow and completed by the Revd J. Christy, who gave his name to nearby Christy's Lane. The porch was originally part of Ashcombe House. In 1894 Belmont House became home to a community of Benedictine priests and student priests from France. After the Benedictines left in 1898, the Sons of Mary Immaculate took over and ran the Church of the Sacred Heart in the house until St Edward's Roman Catholic Church in Salisbury Street opened in 1910. Belmont became a private house again before opening as a hotel in 1924, initially owned by the Johnson family of Shaftesbury. Today's hotel includes a swimming pool to the right of the main building and a ballroom to the left.

Coombe House and St Mary's School

Coombe House, the elegant building that now houses St Mary's School, was built in 1886 as a country home for Mark Hanbury Beaufoy, Liberal MP for Kennington, London, and owner of the Beaufoy Vinegar Brewery at Bermondsey, a business with roots dating back to the 1730s. It was used as a hotel in the 1930s and a rest home for US Air Force personnel towards the end of the Second World War, before becoming St Mary's Convent in 1945.

Coombe House and St Mary's School

The rear view of Coombe House. The slightly lower section (far left) is now the school hall. The school chapel (just out of shot to the right) is among the additions that have appeared since the old picture was taken in the early 1900s. Mark Hanbury Beaufoy would probably approve of his former home's use as a Catholic girls' school, as he actively promoted education and chaired the inaugural meeting of the Waifs and Strays Home in South Lambeth, forerunner of the Children's Society. He also campaigned for the eight-hour working day. *Inset*: The Nun's Well and lake at Coombe around 1905.

Mampitts Lane

East of Christy's Lane and almost opposite Little Firs is Mampitts Lane – a totally rural farm track when this cyclist, children and dog posed for the camera in the early twentieth century, but not any more. Mampitts Farm was sold many years ago and houses, built at various times up to the present day (below), now cover what was once farmland. Shaftesbury Cemetery was opened off Mampitts Lane in 1927, while the old Secondary Modern School stood nearby from the 1950s until it was demolished in 1983. The remains of prehistoric flints and pottery were found in pits in Mampitts Lane in 1949–50.

Little Firs

A road now bisects the grass triangle that graced the junction of Coppice Street and Christy's Lane in the early twentieth century, although the corner known as Little Firs retains much of its greenery. Shaftesbury Youth Club now stands behind the trees. Council houses began to appear at this end of Coppice Street (far left) between the two world wars while Christy's Lane (right) is part of the A350 and one of the town's busiest roads.

Ivy Cross

These Victorian villas at Ivy Cross were built in 1899 and have changed rather less than the surrounding environment, which now includes the busy A350 road outside, a filling station and fast-food outlets opposite and the Ivy Cross roundabout (far left of modern picture).

The Beeches

Still eminently recognisable after more than 100 years is The Beeches, the short link road between Bleke Street and New Road. The Knoll, as the house (right) is known, looks virtually identical but on the opposite corner the ornamental lamp standard has given way to a less elegant telegraph pole and direction sign. The horse droppings in the foreground are a reminder of the transport revolution that was about to unfold in the early twentieth century. The overhanging beech trees that presumably gave this spot its name have long gone.

Pensbury

Lord Portman's hounds meet on the green at Pensbury beside the junction with the Motcombe and Gillingham roads around 1900. The horse-drawn carriage in the foreground advertises baker and confectioner J. H. Pope's Cosy Corner Restaurant in The Commons. Standing in front of the fence (left of centre) are pupils of the nearby Girls' High School. The fence itself looks almost identical today, but the triangular green has been absorbed by the B3081 road. The modern picture was taken from New Road with the A30 flyover behind the camera.

Victoria Street

This terrace of cottages in Victoria Street has changed little since it was built more than a century ago. In 2005 a plaque was unveiled on the wall of one of these houses in the belief that actor Robert Newton, arguably Shaftesbury's most famous son, was born there 100 years earlier as his family passed through the town. It was later removed after it became clear that he was actually born at Cann. Newton, who played Long John Silver in the 1950 Disney film *Treasure Island*, died in 1956 aged just fifty after a long battle against alcoholism. Six nuns ran a private school in one of the houses, Iona, from 1905 to 1908. Homefarris House, which provides sheltered accommodation opposite, takes its name from John Farris's Belle Vue Ironworks (inset above), which formerly stood on the site and was the town's biggest employer with a workforce of more than eighty. Farris built his own home, Llanreath (inset below), at the corner of Bleke Street and Victoria Street where Brionne Garden is today. Hundreds turned out for his funeral in 1914, including town councilors, employees, farmers and business people.

53

Bleke Street and New Road

The flower trough at the junction of Bleke Street and New Road was originally a drinking fountain placed there to refresh travellers who had just climbed the hill from the Gillingham and Motcombe direction. New Road itself (left) was constructed in the nineteenth century to provide a gentler ascent into the town.

Bleke Street Drinking Fountain

The drinking fountain turned flower trough has not only had its function changed but also its position. It is now set against the rear wall. In the background of the *c.* 1910 picture are the walls of the former Girls' High School. Bleke Street was once called Ram Street, but if you stand here in the dead of winter, you may conclude that the current name is more appropriate.

Grosvenor House and Girls' High School

Grosvenor House off Bleke Street dates from 1737 but became a school in the early nineteenth century, when the Revd Thomas Evans opened a private boys' school called the Grosvenor House Academy. His wife later converted it to a girls' school. In 1884 Miss Dunn merged it with her existing school in the High Street to create the Girls' High School, which she ran for forty-one years, catering for both boarders and day pupils. Miss Dunn offered a high standard of education and a wide range of subjects and required an equally high standard of appearance from her pupils. These pictures are from one of Miss Dunn's promotional brochures. The school later became Shaftesbury High School for Girls.

Grosvenor House and Girls' High School

Before its closure in 1983, the Girls' High School occupied much of what is now the town's central car park. The site of classrooms and netball court (above) today offers long-stay parking. The main buildings (below) are now business premises and flats with parking in the courtyard. Former pupil Sarah Mayo, who now works in the building as a secretary with architects Proctor Watts Cole Rutter, recalls that by the end of the school's life, some floors were in such poor condition that pupils were told to 'sit down and not move' for fear of something giving way.

Old Market Entrance, Bleke Street

The Bleke Street entrance to Shaftesbury's main car park was once the entrance to the cattle market. The rings used to tie up cattle can still be seen on some of the car park's walls (right of pictures). The house on the left in the background was once a boarding house for the Girls' High School across the road and later the Sunridge Hotel before becoming La Fleur de Lys Hotel a few years ago.

Livestock Market, 1907 and Today
In 1902 John Jeffery and his father opened their Shaftesbury livestock market on what is now the car park site between Bleke Street and Bell Street. The market became well known for its sale of barren cows. The above picture shows the 'Prize Barrener Sale' in 1907. The market moved to its present Christy's Lane site in 1956. It was officially opened by Shaftesbury's Jack Young, 'the oldest farmer in the district', and John Whitehead, of Glastonbury, both of whom had been sending cattle to the market for more than fifty years.

Bell Street United Church

Today's Bell Street United Church at the corner of Bell Street and Parsons Pool has a long history, for this site was once occupied by St Laurence's, one of Shaftesbury's dozen medieval churches. It became Shaftesbury Methodist Church in 1766, as confirmed by the date stone high on the gable wall. It was rebuilt in 1827 and again – for safety reasons – in 1907, and the date stone was transferred on both occasions. Tradition has it that John Wesley, the founder of Methodism, opened the first chapel in 1766 during one of his sixteen visits to Shaftesbury. Below, a large crowd gathers for the laying of the foundation stone ahead of the 1907 rebuild. Much of the stone from the 1827 building was reused with some additional Bath stone for the facings and windows.

Bell Street United Church

The Wesleyan Church and the view along Parsons Pool following the 1907 rebuild and today. In 1907 it was renamed the Charles Garratt Memorial Church in honour of a Shaftesbury-born preacher, who founded the Liverpool mission and became president of the Methodist Conference. The Edwardian building is architecturally less severe than its nineteenth-century forbear, although it still harks back to an earlier era. In the distant days of St Laurence's Church, Bell Street was known as St Laurence's Street. The street took its present name from a long-lost pub called the Bell.

Corner of Bell Street and Parsons Pool

Parsons Pool takes its name from what historian John Hutchins described as a 'kind of reservoir for rainwater used for washing houses'. By the late seventeenth century the pool at the east corner of Parsons Pool and Bell Street had given way to Fricker's bakehouse, which caught fire in 1707 but was still a bakery when the above picture was taken about 170 years later. The Smith family replaced the old building with the present one in 1885. By the 1970s it had become a health food shop called Helianthe (below).

Corner of Bell Street and Parsons Pool

By the First World War, Smith's the bakers had become C. J. Stretch & Sons, grocers, confectioners and bakers. Their Ford Model T delivery vans can be seen outside while the shop windows advertise 'Cadbury's Chocolate, Bournville Cocoa and Rowntree's Cocoa'. A newspaper advertisement dated 1919 promises that orders will be 'promptly attended to'. Alderman Charles Job Stretch was a magistrate and mayor of Shaftesbury in 1921, 1922 and 1936. The shop's latest incarnation is Bright Blooms Floral Boutique (below). The barber shop (left) has been there for many years.

Corner of Bell Street and Mustons Lane

The former antiques shop Mr Punch's Market on the corner of Bell Street and Mustons Lane has changed little in appearance since it was an upholsterer's more than 100 years ago. In the 1980s it was a record shop called Trax (inset), selling 'CDs, tapes, LPs and singles', according to the sign. It now stores agricultural equipment.

Old Police Station, Bell Street

Although there are plenty of other people hanging around but no policemen in sight, the second building on the right in this Bell Street picture was Shaftesbury police station in the early twentieth century. We can just see the light above the front door. The public library now stands on that site. All that remains of the police station are the painted railing posts with crowns on top. Part of the building nearest the camera (right) was once used as a military drill hall. It now houses the First Start Nursery, Pre-school and Holiday Club, with the more recent public library building next door.

Bell Street

This view looks south-west along Bell Street from the junction with Angel Lane. The house on the left retains the same ornamental porch, windows and chimney pots that it had more than 100 years ago. A blue plaque tells us that between around 1757 and 1870, this was the site of William Lush's Blue Coat School, which 'gave free education, clothes and apprenticeships to poor boys'. It is now called The Retreat and offers bed and breakfast.

Kings Arms

The Kings Arms adjoining the old market site in Bleke Street is said to have been built using stone from the abbey ruins, which would date it from the sixteenth or seventeenth centuries. In 1681 it featured in a corruption investigation after Thomas Barney, the Poole Surveyor of Customs, tracked twenty-two packets of smuggled cloth to the pub. According to a Treasury report, the notoriously corrupt Barney accepted a bribe from the merchant involved and let the matter drop, claiming that 'the King's duties was paid at Weymouth'. Blandford brewers Hall and Woodhouse bought the pub in 1924 and the older picture was taken soon after.

Old Ship Hotel

At one time Shaftesbury boasted more than fifty pubs, prompting Thomas Hardy to comment that beer was more plentiful than water in the hilltop town, adding that there were also 'more wanton women than honest wives and maids'. Two of those pubs have been called the Ship. The Ship Hotel (above, *c.* 1900) stood opposite the Bimport turning, where public toilets and the corner of the short-stay car park are today. The building that was to become the Ship Inn can be seen in the background. The premises nearer the camera – signed 'Garage' in the old photograph – survive as a teddy bear shop and a Polish store. Across the road, the corner shop that was Strange Brothers, grocers, in 1900 has had many incarnations across 430 years. Lord Arundel built a town house there in around 1590. It later became another of the fifty pubs, the Rose & Crown. More recently, it was a youth centre called Toby's Court and at the time of writing was being converted for use as a fish and chip shop.

Ship Inn and Avishayes

The Ship Inn at the top of Tout Hill is thought to be one of the oldest pubs, possibly dating back to 1514. It has also been known as the Ram and the Half Moon. In the early twentieth century it was the surgery of Dr Harris, who lived next door in a house called Avishays (right in both pictures – and sometimes spelt Avishayes). Dr Harris was one of three wealthy residents who literally bought most of Shaftesbury in 1919. This kindly GP also attended the confinements of gipsy women, thus keeping them out of the dreaded workhouse, and helped convalescing boys by taking them on his rounds in his pony and trap or red motorcar. Avishays was also the last home of Elizabeth Pepperell (died 1971), whose tireless efforts to improve the rights of women in the workplace earned her the OBE. Called Pepperell House, it is now an Abbeyfield home, providing sheltered accommodation for the elderly.

Holy Trinity Church, Bimport

There has been a church on the Bimport site since at least 1302, when it was associated with the nunnery, but the present Holy Trinity building dates from 1841 to 1842. The Grade II-listed building was Shaftesbury's main church before it was deconsecrated in 1974. Five or six years later it was converted to other uses, including offices, a day-care centre and a scout hall. The tower is one of the highest buildings in Dorset and can be seen from miles around. Part of the extensive churchyard has been stripped of grass and gravestones to create forty parking spaces. The churchyard is also known for its lime trees and is a good place to see snowdrops early in the year. The two bells at the entrance to Gold Hill Museum are from Holy Trinity.

Savoy Cinema and Savoy Court, Bimport

Pictures of the Savoy Cinema in Bimport are surprisingly scarce, but we've managed to come up with three, including two (inset above and below) taken at the point of demolition in the mid-1980s. The Savoy opened in July 1933 with an invitation matinee attended by the mayor, Corporation and other dignitaries, followed by an evening showing of *Maid of the Mountains* to the wider public. Admission was 9*d*, 1*s* 3*d* and 1*s* 6*d*. One of the last films shown there in 1983 was *E.T. the Extra-Terrestrial*. The Savoy survived to see its fiftieth anniversary and briefly became a bingo hall before final closure and demolition. A large apartment block called Savoy Court now occupies the site.

Old Gasworks and Ambulance Station, Bimport

The present ambulance station site in Bimport was once the home of Shaftesbury Gasworks, established in 1836 and the scene of a drama in May 1854, when the gasholder exploded so violently that people thought there had been an earthquake. Holy Trinity Church was one of several buildings that suffered damage but no one was injured and fears that fire could spread to other parts of the town proved unfounded. The privately owned gasworks were uninsured. The explosion is one of three theories to explain a large hole or cavern that is said to exist beneath the ambulance station car park. It could also be the brick cavern in which the gasholder floated or the remains of a well dating from the heyday of Shaftesbury Abbey. Although the showroom and offices remained in Bimport until the post-war decades, the later gasholders were erected between Castle Hill and Enmore Green. The last of these can be seen towards the left of the c. 1955 aerial picture (above). Below, paramedic Steve White tests his emergency lights.

Gasholders, Castle Hill and Bimport

Directors and staff line up for a photograph on Shaftesbury's penultimate gasholder, which stood near the foot of Castle Hill. The girders on four sides stood on runners, which enabled the holder to rise and fall as it was filled with gas or emptied. The last two gasholders stood almost side by side for many years in the mid-twentieth century but the older one became redundant after the top became rusted. The top made a tempting target for stone-throwing children on Castle Hill. In his book, Fred Long tells an amusing story of former gasworks manager Mr E. Yates, who told a fellow Shastonian George Thick that he must be drinking heavily as his nose was so red. 'My nose is like your gas meters – registers more than it consumes,' Thick shot back. *Inset*: an early Shaftesbury gasholder as featured on the gas company's letterhead.

Gasworkers' Cottages, Bimport

After the gasworks was established in 1836, the terrace of cottages with gable-shaped canopies (left) was built alongside to house the manager, workers and their families. The cottages have changed little since then, although there is rarely (if ever) a time when there are not cars parked outside. Before John Jeffery & Son opened their livestock market off Bleke Street in 1902, Bimport doubled as Shaftesbury's sheep and cattle market.

Bimport

Looking west along Bimport towards the top of St John's Hill in the early 1900s, the gasworkers' cottages can be seen to the right. Meanwhile, the tower of Holy Trinity Church affords a fine view (below) of Bimport and the Blackmore Vale beyond. The cars were parked on Castle Hill for the Gold Hill Fair. The house with the jutting porch (far right) has a blue plaque reminding us that it featured as Old Grove Place in Thomas Hardy's novel *Jude the Obscure*. Six centuries ago Bimport was the northern frontage of the abbey complex, lined with stables and storage buildings including granary, wool house and larder house with courtyards behind. The sole survivor from the nunnery days is the central part of Edwardstowe (inset above), a range of cottages near where Bimport meets St John's Hill. Built around 1500, it is Shaftesbury's oldest house.

Castle Hill

Generations of Shaftesbury visitors and residents have enjoyed sitting on Castle Hill and admiring the views to the north and north-west. On a clear day you can see Somerset's Quantock Hills 43 miles away, the Mendips 30 miles away and Glastonbury Tor 24 miles distant. In the early days of the abbey, the streets of Saxon Shaftesbury were on Castle Hill and there is thought to be much archaeology beneath the soil. The present town centre to the east of the abbey was established in the eleventh century.

Enmore Green

Enmore Green looking towards Tout Hill in the early 1900s and a somewhat closer view today. The cream-coloured building to the right of the modern picture (and second right of the old one) was the Fountain Inn, which closed as this book was in preparation. The pub was so called because Enmore Green's springs once supplied Shaftesbury with much of its water, which was hauled up steep Tout Hill by horses and donkeys.

Enmore Green from Castle Hill

The slopes of Castle Hill have seen a fair amount of tree growth in the century or so between the taking of these two pictures, while the number of houses in Enmore Green, the village at the foot of the hill, has multiplied. Gabled extensions have also been added to the older cottages in the foreground.

Enmore Green from Castle Hill

Enmore Green viewed from a different angle showing the extent of development in the last 100 years. The prominent building to the left is the Methodist church, now a private house. The old postcard is postmarked 1911 and the sender appears to be notifying the recipient of a football result: Shaftesbury 6 Okeford 1. The author's maternal grandfather, Jim Ridout, played for Okeford Fitzpaine in the early 1900s and would not have enjoyed this scoreline.

The Old Parsonage, Tout Hill
This view looks down Tout Hill with the Old Parsonage on the right. The two sets of stone steps linking the raised footpath to the road have been partly eroded by generations of Shaftesbury feet. The lower set is usually partially obscured by parked cars today. Tout Hill was also known as the Old Coach Road, as it once formed part of the Great West Road between London and the West Country.

The Old Parsonage and Tout Hill House

Tout Hill was once one of the most challenging sections of the Great West Road and extra horses were needed to pull the coaches up the steep incline. In 1817 the hill was widened and the gradient made less severe, a task that involved removing and rebuilding part of the old boundary wall on the west side. *Below and inset*: Tout Hill House stands about halfway up the hill and its bay windows, though now partly obscured by vegetation, are readily recognisable.

Union Workhouse

It's a modern bungalow development today but a century ago Umbers Hill off Breach Lane was occupied by the Shaftesbury Union Workhouse, which accepted paupers from not only the town itself but Gillingham and many villages. The building was demolished in around 1952 and barely a trace remains today apart from the brick entrance splay, which has been filled in, and a section of the old nurses' quarters and washroom, which survive as a single-storey bungalow called Valley Cottage (below).

Workhouse from Breach Lane

The typically austere workhouse can be seen in the background as three young ladies, a baby and a dog pose for a picture in the field on the other side of Breach Lane. The same shot today shows the bungalow development in Umbers Hill and the field transformed into the community farm and allotments known as Shaftesbury Home Grown.

St John's Hill and View of St James's

The above postcard showing St John's Hill with Cliff House on the right and St James's Church in the background is postmarked 1923, but the photograph was probably taken a couple of decades earlier, as the house behind the wall on the left is thought to have been built in the early 1900s. The house is called Ethelgiva after a daughter of King Alfred, who became Shaftesbury's first abbess. Ethelgiva the house (inset) obscures the view of St James's but a fine view can still be had a few yards back up the hill (below). St John's Church, another of Shaftesbury's many long-lost churches, stood to the right of St John's Hill looking down. It was said to have been one of the few churches in England where the churchyard (which survives with many damaged stones) was higher than the tower.

St John's Hill Crossroads
St John's Hill's crossroads with Tanyard Lane (left), Breach Lane (right) and St James's Church in the background. In the modern picture the church is largely hidden behind the trees. The dog-walker agreed to pose with his pet for the camera on the same spot occupied by the woman and child more than a century ago.

Old St James's Church

St James's Church was not only rebuilt in 1867 but slightly relocated so that it now stands further from the road that skirts the churchyard rather than adjacent to it. The old church (above and below) was said to have a nave that was not square with its chancel and side walls that were 'slanting very much'.

St James's Church, Early 1900s and Today
St James's Church a century ago (above) and today (below). The 150th anniversary of the present church's dedication was celebrated in July 2017.

St James's Street Fire

A major fire took place on 17 June 1955 after a painter working with a blowtorch at No. 77 St James's Street accidentally set fire to the thatch beneath the galvanised iron sheeting that covered the roofs of a long terrace of cottages. A strong south-east wind fanned the flames and six adjoining cottages were soon engulfed. The fifty Dorset and Wiltshire firemen who fought the blaze included James Parsons, who lived in one of the cottages affected, No. 79, and his uncle, Charles Parsons, Shaftesbury's Chief Station Officer. Most of St James's 300 residents formed a human chain to rescue furniture and other possessions, most of which were saved and stored in the school and church hall.

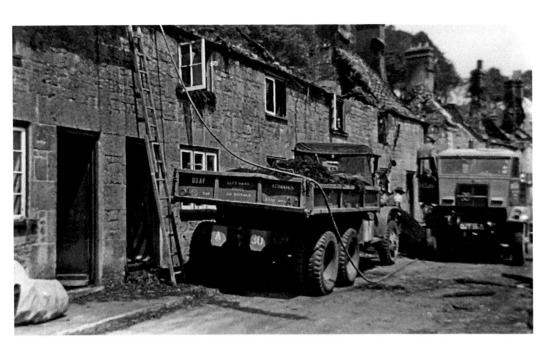

St James's Street Fire

Kathleen Heasman, whose parents Mr and Mrs C. J. Rapley lived at No. 77, was among the first on the scene and recalls that men from the US Air Force stationed at Guys Marsh helped to fight the fire and clear up the debris, although their firefighting was hindered because their hoses didn't fit with the local hydrants. A USAF lorry can be seen in the above picture. The firefighting was hampered by a shortage of water and firemen had to run hoses hundreds of yards to augment the supply. The cottages were fully repaired (below) but with tiles rather than thatch and galvanised iron.

St James's Street and the Fox and Hounds Looking North-east

When the above picture was taken in the early 1900s, the second house on the left was the Fox and Hounds pub. The couple in the centre may be the landlord and landlady with their two youngest children. Many other youngsters have joined them for the photo shoot along with the chimney sweep, who is standing at the corner of Tanyard Lane. Below, a similar view today.

St James's Street and the Fox and Hounds Looking South-west

A view looking along St James's Street towards the church with the Fox and Hounds and the Tanyard Lane junction near right. The pub closed in the 1950s and is now a private dwelling. Like most of its neighbours, it has also lost its thatched roof in favour of tiles, but the porch overhang (foreground) survives.

St James's Street and Hand in Hand

Another of St James's Street's old pubs was the Hand in Hand, which stood next to the Pump Yard (left side of street). Shaftesbury historian Brenda Innes suggests that the pub may have taken its name from a friendly society, as the property appears on earlier deeds as 'club houses'. The people in the street in the early 1900s picture include two men and a boy armed with a shovel, roller and wheelbarrow, so were perhaps doing some road repairs or gardening. The pub closed several decades ago but lives on through the building's current name, Hand in Hand Cottage. It is the last in the terrace of white cottages.

Pump Yard

With its pump at the centre of a courtyard and cottages on three sides, Pump Yard is a unique and picturesque corner of Shaftesbury and a magnet to artists and photographers. It wasn't always that pretty. It used to be known as Andrews' Yard after one-time owner James Andrews, and has been described as an 'insanitary warren of airless cottages'. In the nineteenth century Earl Grosvenor (later Marquis of Westminster) demolished the front cottages and replaced the others with buildings of a higher standard.

Ye Olde Two Brewers

Ye Olde Two Brewers Inn near the foot of Gold Hill is the only survivor of at least five pubs that once graced St James's Street. Three of them are remembered in an old saying that 'the Old Two Brewers walked Hand in Hand to the Fox and Hounds'. The other pubs were the White Hart and the Ben of Leather, so called because its customers included workers from the tanneries hereabouts. Ye Olde Two Brewers today advertises itself in large letters across its roof (below). These four pictures show the pub in four eras spanning 120 years. The picture with the car is probably from the 1920s while the lower one opposite shows former landlord Harold 'Knocker' Case and his wife Betty in the 1960s. Knocker was formerly landlord of the Lamb at Ludwell and the Kings Arms at Shaftesbury – although he allegedly spent more time drinking in other people's pub than working in his own.

Ye Olde Two Brewers

In *Tales of Old Shaftesbury*, Fred Long describes another former Two Brewers landlord, Seymour Usher, who was 'mine host' for fifty years and quite a character. 'In his younger days, he was a trick violinist and played in some of the London Music Halls,' says Long. 'He had a pony which went on the stage with him and Seymour would play the violin using the pony's tail instead of a bow. His stage name was Leslie St Marr.' Seymour also kept a talking parrot, which escaped one morning prompting a massive search. When the bird was eventually found perched on a wall at Holyrood Farm, it calmly announced: 'Good morning.' Seymour's ostler, Fred Oborne, grabbed the bird and told it, 'You wait till I get you back in your cage. I'll tell you something!'

Gold Hill Museum and St Peter's Church

The Town Hall, St Peter's Church tower and, in the foreground, the Gold Hill Museum in around 1960 and today, pictured from the museum's award-winning cottage garden. The museum is owned by the Shaftesbury and District Historical Society and managed by volunteers. The society was formed in 1946 and soon after was allowed to use a room at the Town Hall for its fledgling museum. As its collection rapidly expanded, it moved into a cottage on Gold Hill. In 1957 it moved into its present premises at Nos 1 and 2 Gold Hill. In 2011, with help from a Heritage Lottery Fund grant, the museum renovated and extended the building. The building dates at least from the fifteenth century and has previously been a priest's house, which still has a 'squint' through the wall into St Peter's Church, an old lodging house for traders attending the market in Gold Hill and an inn called the Sun & Moon. The majority of historic pictures in this book have been drawn from the museum's collection along with much of the information in the extended captions.